Dollys and Friends
Originals

Color, Cut, Dress Up

1920s Paper Dolls

Coloring Book

Dollys and Friends
Originals

Dolly

Lolly

Jolly

Molly

Holly

Polly

Meet Dolly, Polly, Holly, Lolly, Jolly and Molly, new fashion paper dolls Dollys and
Friends. You can begin creating your collection of paper dolls with this book
which has 3 paper dolls and more than 40 outfits. With this coloring book you get to
decide on the color of their outfits, and create unique wardrobe pieces.
If you like the coloring book version you may also like
their full colored paper dolls collections.

Paper doll lovers and coloring enthusiasts of all ages will find hours of entertainment
with more than 40 pieces of vintage style outfits. If you want your creations to last
longer; color the outfit pages and then glue them to card stock before cutting. This
book includes an extra copy of each of the outfits, so you can try different colors
and combinations, or have a back-up in case of an error you made.

Please be aware that these paper dolls require careful hand cutting. For adults, paper
dolls may be a gateway to childhood memories but they also make great gifts for
children. Younger children may need the help to cut these dolls out since the dolls and
clothes are not perforated. However, this is a nice opportunity for fun family time.
Paper dolls can bring adults and children together, and collections of paper dolls have
always passed down to younger generations. New generations can learn a lot while
playing with paper dolls. In a digital era where dress up games allow us to change
clothes on paper dolls by only touching a screen, cutting these dolls the traditional way
is a great help for developing motor skills. Playing together also helps to develop
communication and cooperation between friends and family. Playing games goes hand
in hand with storytelling, role-playing and fantasy so everyone can treasure the time
spent playing with these paper dolls as memories full of creativity and imagination.

Paper dolls have a long history, and although inspired by antique and vintage paper
dolls, Dollys and Friends are modern fashion dolls. Still, most of their wardrobe pieces
are vintage fashions or period costumes. While these clothes are created after research,
each outfit may not be authentic for that time period. Although there are many
costumes and designer fashions for vintage themed books, it is still best to describe
them as inspired by historical periods but not exact period costumes. Especially
undergarments are more modern for the dolls to be used with different wardrobe
choices. Every new outfit from Dollys and Friends Originals Books you will get will
be wearable by these Original Dollys. Collecting these paper dolls
and sharing them with children
can also make fashion and history become one of their passions.

As an illustrator with a background in fashion design,
I had hours of fun drawing the Dollys.
I really hope that paper doll fans and children of all ages
enjoy these creations as much as I did.
I wish everyone who is coloring, cutting out these dolls and trying the outfits
has a great time with this entertaining activity.

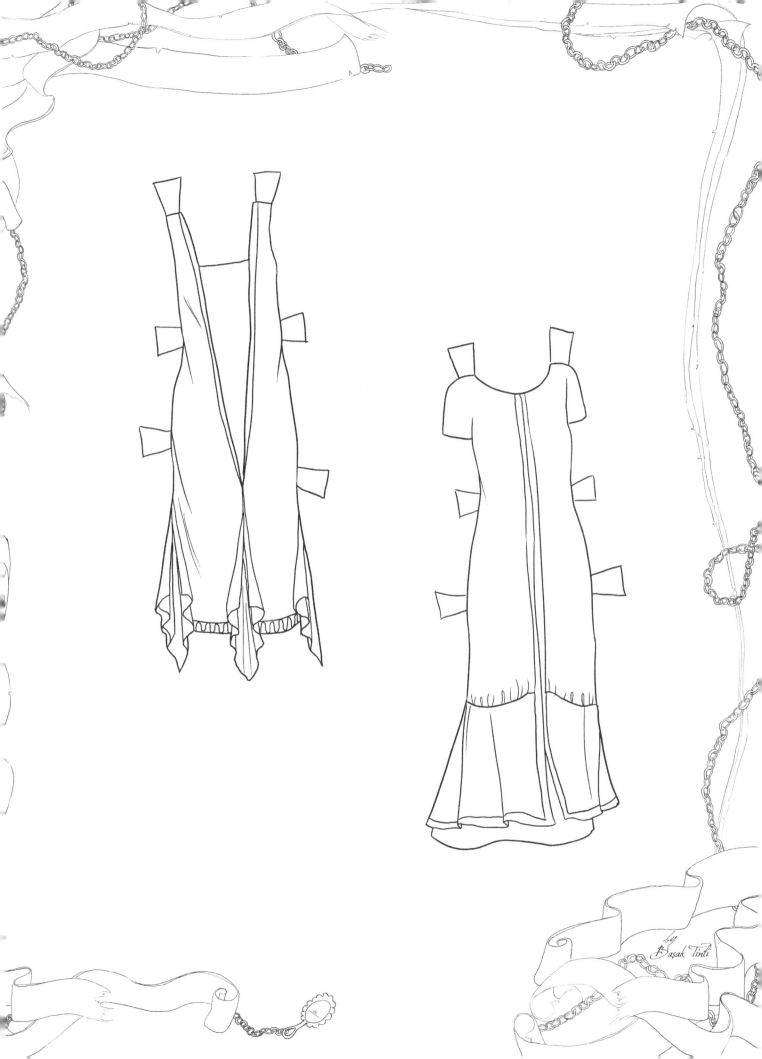

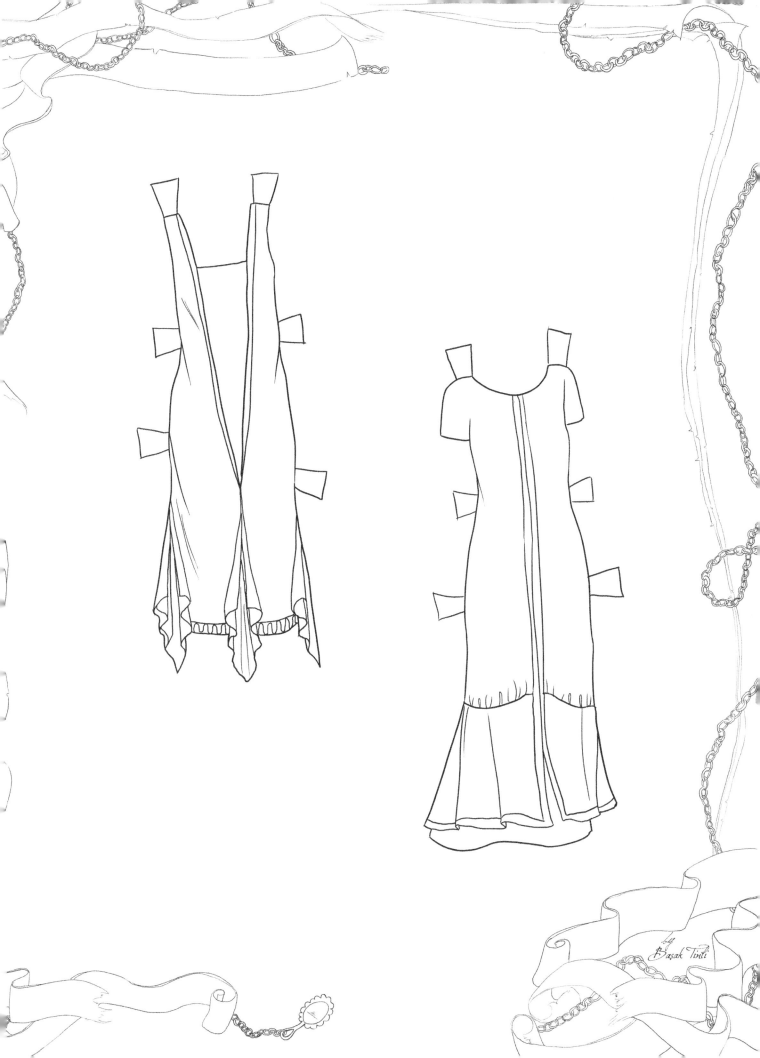

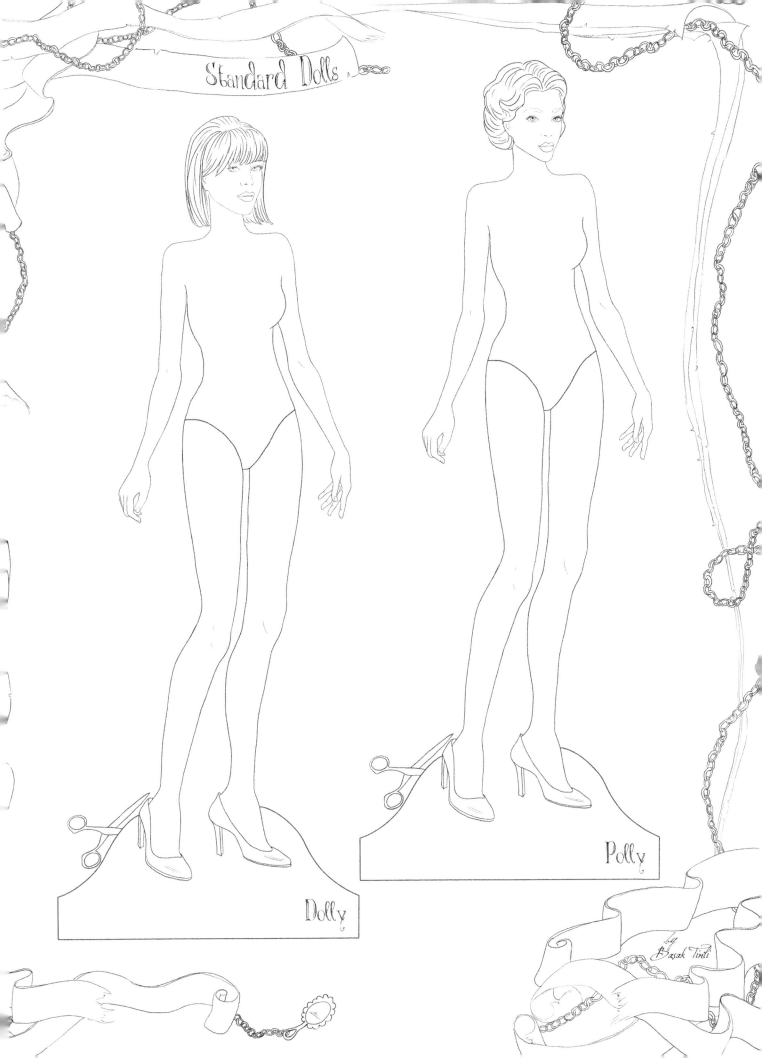

Standard Dolls

Dolly

Polly

Standard Dolls

Holly

Lolly

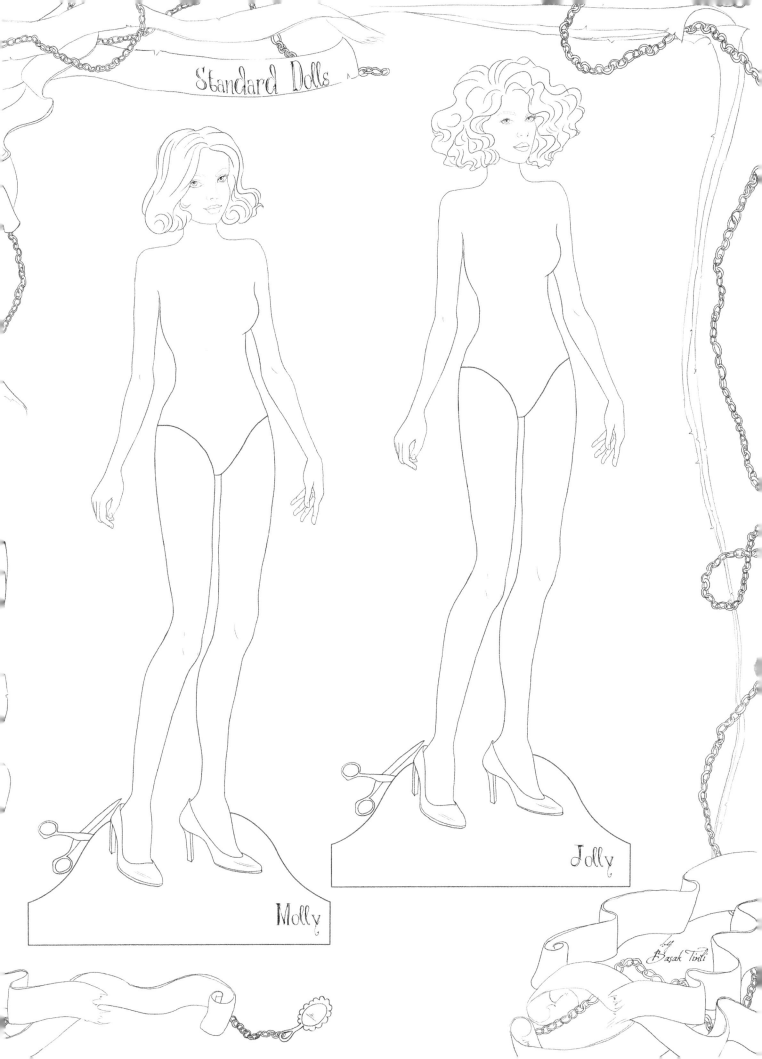

Standard Dolls

Molly

Jolly

by Başak Tinli

Made in the USA
Monee, IL
19 October 2020